BRANCH LINES TO NEWQUAY

Vic Mitchell and Keith Smith

MP Middleton Press

Cover picture: Prairie tank no. 5526 leaves St. Blazey with a typical local train of the 1950s. The two first class compartments of the 7.55pm Par to Newquay are over the River Par on 5th July 1955. (R.C.Riley / Transport Treasury)

Published October 2001

ISBN 1 901706 71 0

© Middleton Press, 2001

Design   David Pede
Typesetting   Barbara Mitchell

Published by
            Middleton Press
            Easebourne Lane
            Midhurst, West Sussex
            GU29 9AZ
Tel: 01730 813169
Fax: 01730 812601

Printed & bound by Biddles Ltd,
            Guildford and Kings Lynn

CONTENTS

1. From Par 1-61   2. From Chacewater 62-103   3. Newquay Area 104-120

INDEX

ACKNOWLEDGEMENTS

In addition to those mentioned in the credits, we would like to thank most sincerely the following for assistance so generously given: L.Crosier, G.Croughton, E.W.Fry, F.Hornby, K.Jenkin, R.A.Lumber, L.W.Rowe, Mr D. and Dr S. Salter, G.T.V.Stacey, E.Wilmshurst, R.Winnen, E.Youldon and as always, our wives.

I.   The 1947 Railway Clearing House map includes four mineral-only branches south of the Par-Newquay line, but none of the halts on the Chacewater-Newquay route.

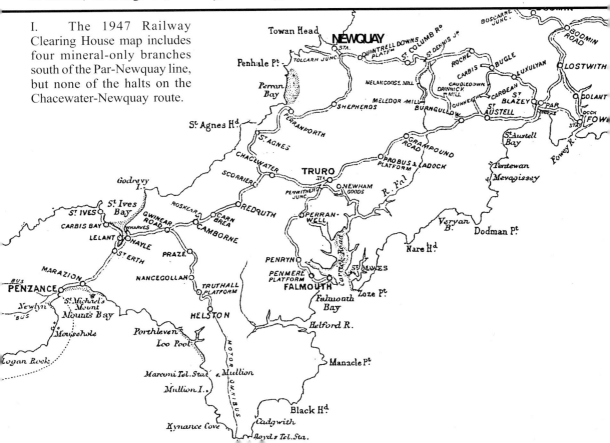

GEOGRAPHICAL SETTING

From Par

The village of Par is situated north of the busy harbour, which specialises in china clay export. It is at the mouth of the River Par, which drains Red Moor and which has formed a deeply incised valley along which the branch climbs for about two miles.

The next four miles or so are on or near Granite, the products of decomposition of which include china clay, a commodity of great economic value to the district. The associated waste after extraction has been formed into conical mounds, many of which have become green and no longer present white lesions in the landscape. The industry continues to generate substantial rail traffic, much of the output being used in paper making and not china.

The climb ends on Goss Moor, an infertile and desolate area nearly 500ft above sea level. A steady descent follows to the popular seaside resort of Newquay, where the terminus is 100ft above sea level. Its harbour is no longer of commercial importance for transport.

From Chacewater

This route starts at an altitude of about 400ft and climbs mainly over farmland to reach the station serving the picturesque settlement of St. Agnes. A steep descent takes the route almost down to sea level at the charming coastal resort of Perranporth. A severe climb takes the alignment over the high ground of Newlyn Downs before the route descends across pastoral scenery and along the Lappa Valley to reach Newquay.

The line was laid almost entirely on Old Red Sandstone.

The maps herein are to the scale of 25ins to 1 mile, unless otherwise indicated.

II.

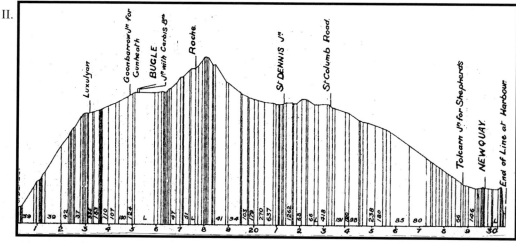

III.

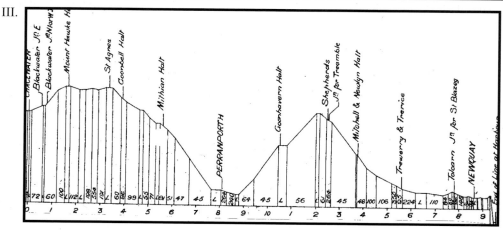

HISTORICAL BACKGROUND

The Par Canal was built between 1833 and 1838 and extended inland to serve mines for copper and iron, plus several clay pits. This was part of a larger scheme developed by Mr J.A.Treffry, a local landowner and industrialist, who completed Par Harbour in 1840. He acquired Newquay Harbour and set about linking it with clay works and iron mines by means of a tramway. A line from the south reached Colcerrow Quarry in 1841 and by 1843 it had been extended to Luxulyan and Molinnis. Traffic included tin, lead, granite and china clay downwards and coal, timber and lime upwards. The Molinnis to Pontsmill section opened in 1847.

The Treffry Tramway was standard gauge and was worked by horses, excepting the rope-worked incline. Work started at Newquay in 1845, but the line was not completed until 1849 and then only to a point near St. Dennis. Another tramway was built southward from Newquay to East Wheal Rose and it opened in February 1849.

The Cornwall Railway opened from Plymouth to Truro on 2nd May 1859, but the tracks were broad gauge. The Truro to Redruth section was laid to standard gauge by the West Cornwall Railway and opened in 1852. This was later relaid to broad gauge, but all Cornish lines were standard gauge by 1892, by which time the main lines were part of the Great Western Railway.

The Cornish Minerals Railway was formed in 1872 to lease the Treffry Tramways, complete the missing section, eliminate the canal, replace the inclines with new alignments and upgrade the track for use by locomotives. The Act of Incorporation was passed on 21st July 1873 and this included an extension to Fowey from Par. About 2½ miles of the line in the Luxulyan Valley was on a new alignment and a locomotive works was built at St. Blazey. A branch from the East Wheal Rose line was laid to Treamble and on to Gravel Hill.

Freight traffic commenced between Fowey and Newquay on 1st June 1874, but iron-mining was in terminal decline and there was a slump in the china clay business. Grasping at straws, the impoverished CMR hired some coaches and started a passenger service on an unrecorded date in 1876. The GWR took over the operation of the line from 1st October 1877 and also some mineral branches which are not included in this volume.

The GWR laid double track between Par and St. Blazey and opened it on 1st January 1879. There was no through running, as its main line remained broad gauge until May 1892. The CMR was purchased outright by the GWR in 1896.

The GWR did much to develop the holiday trade in Cornwall with the opening of the Chacewater to Perranporth section on 6th July 1903, Perranporth to Newquay on 2nd January 1905 and the introduction of direct through coaches from London to Newquay in May 1906.

Doubling of the Par-Newquay line was undertaken thus: St. Dennis to Tregoss Moor in 1921, Goonbarrow Junction to Bugle in 1930 and Tolcarn Junction to Newquay in 1940-46.

Nationalisation in 1948 resulted in few changes locally. Eventually however, British Railways closed the Chacewater-Newquay section, this taking effect for passengers and freight on 4th February 1963.

Privatisation changes in the mid-1990s resulted in most trains on the remaining branch being operated by Wales & West from 13th October 1996, the franchise being for 7½ years.

PASSENGER SERVICES

Par to Newquay

The first timetables showed two weekday trains and one on Sundays. The latter was soon dropped; all originated at Fowey. From 1879 the new curve meant that trains started from Par instead, three per day, weekdays only.

The timetable for 1893 showed five journeys. The 1906 issue included seven and was the first to have a through train from London; it stopped only twice on the branch. A similar service was still being offered in the Summer of 1914.

The basic frequency had increased to eight by 1938 and nine by 1947. The 1955 timetable in the Summer offered ten on Mondays to Fridays, but 22 on Saturdays and six on Sundays. Terminal points for the Saturday extras included Bristol, London (5), Plymouth, York, Wolverhampton, Manchester and Newcastle.

By 1966, cuts meant that there were only four through trains on Saturdays, the local service being little changed. This type of pattern persisted into the 1980s, but by 1990 the basic service was provided by one DMU, which meant a maximum of six trips Mondays to Fridays and Sundays. On Saturdays there were through trains only, not stopping along the branch. This type of service was still being provided in 2001. These comments relate to the Summer, usually there being no Sunday trains in the Winter.

Chacewater to Newquay

The initial timetable to Perranporth (only) showed six trains daily, the 2.24pm arrival originating at Camborne. When the line was complete, there were ten trips each way daily, but two did not run south of St. Agnes.

The 1914 service comprised seven from Chacewater, one from Penzance and one from Redruth, but weekdays only. This dropped to a simple shuttle service of six trains by 1922, increasing to eight by 1938 and nine by 1947.

The 1955 Summer timetable showed eleven weekday trains, two of which originated at Falmouth. There were seven on Sundays, plus one from Paddington to Perranporth on Saturdays.

The final Summer timetable offered nine weekday and three Sunday trips, most running to and from Truro.

1904

1906

1914

1914

Miles	Down.	m	mrn	m	mrn	m	aft	m	m	aft	m			
	Truro .... dep.	7 43	c	9y55	11 56	2g23	3n25	4y25	d	6 16	8 50	....	....	....
5½	Chacewater .... arr.	7 54	....	10g7	12 9	2g36	3n38	4y38	....	6 29	9 6	....	....	....
–	24 PENZANCE .... dep.	6 35	8 55	9 20	10b35	1b15	2 0	3 0	....	4 30	6 20	....	....	....
–	Chacewater ¶ .... dep.	7 55	....	10 25	12 32	2 43	3 44	4 57	....	6 30	9 7	....	....	....
8½	St. Agnes	8 5	1012	10 35	12 43	2 53	3 54	5 7	6 22	6 41	9 17	....	....	....
3¾	Perranporth .... arr.	8 18	1022	10 51	12 53	3 6	4 6	5 20	6 35	6 51	9 30	....	....	....
	Perranporth .... dep.	8 19	1023	10 52	12 54	3 7	4 7	....	6 36	6 52	9 31	....	....	....
7¾	Shepherds	8 32	1035	11 8	1 6	3 20	4 21	....	6 50	7 4	9 45	....	....	....
3¾	Newquay ¶ *(below)* .... arr.	8 48	1048	11 23	1 19	3 36	4 36	....	7 7	7 19	10 2	....	....	....

Miles	Up.	m	m	mrn	m	aft	aft	m	aft	m	aft		
	Newquay ¶ .... dep.	7 50	8 53	10 50	1 30	2 35	4 8	4 55	....	7 16	8 15	....	....
6	Shepherds	8 6	9 9	11 8	1 46	2 50	4 22	5 11	....	7 32	8 30	....	....
0¼	Perranporth .... arr.	8 25	9 19	11 19	1 55	3 6	4 32	5 23	....	7 41	8 41	....	....
	Perranporth .... dep.	8 26	9 20	11 20	1 56	3 7	4 33	5 24	5 50	7 42	8 42	....	....
5¼	St. Agnes	8 43	9 37	11 35	2 13	3 22	4 48	5 41	6 6	7 59	8 57	....	....
8¾	Chacewater ¶ 20, 24 .... arr.	8 53	9 48	11 46	2 23	3 33	4 56	d	6 15	8 11	c	....	....
9	20 PENZANCE .... arr.	10b33	11 15	1 10	3 35	5 0	7h10	....	9 14	....	10 0	....	....
–	Chacewater .... dep.	8g59	9 52	12n14	2 41	....	5 0	....	6n17	8 14	....	....	....
3¾	Truro .... arr.	9g10	10 3	12n25	2 52	....	5 10	....	6n29	8 27	....	....	....

"Halts" at Mount Hawke, between Chacewater and St. Agnes; Goonbell and Mithian, between St. Agnes and Perranporth; Goonhavern, between Perranporth and Shepherds; and Mitchell and Newlyn and Trewerry and Trerice, between Shepherds and Newquay.

NOTES.

b Via Truro.
c Through Trains to and from Penzance.
d Through Trains to and from Redruth.
g By Train, 1st & 3rd class.
h Via Truro. Arrives at 6 30 aft. on and after 17th instant.
m Motor Car, one class only.
n Motor Car, one class only.

☞ **Other Trains** between Truro and Chacewater page 20.

PAR, ST. BLAZEY, and NEWQUAY.—Great Western.

Miles	Down.	mrn	mrn	mrn	aft	aft	aft (Commences on 17th inst.)	aft	aft					
	Par .... dep.	6 0	9 15	1125	1 50	3 10	4 56	5 30	8 0	....	....	....	....	....
¾	St. Blazey	6 4	9 22	1129	1 55	3 14	....	5 34	8 5	....	....	....	....	....
4½	Luxulyan	n	9 36	1150	2 6	3 25	....	5 45	8 18	....	....	....	....	....
6½	Bugle	....	9 41	1156	2 11	3 30	n	5 50	8 24	....	....	....	....	....
8¾	Roche	6 34	9 48	12 2	2 19	3 40	n	5 58	8 30	....	....	....	....	....
4¼	St. Columb Road ‡	7 0	10 2	1218	2 33	3 53	5 32	6 13	8 45	....	....	....	....	....
8¼	Quintrel Downs Platform	....	1012	1228	2 43	4 3	....	6 23	8 55	....	....	....	....	....
0¾	Newquay † *(above)* .... arr.	7 19	1018	1235	2 49	4 12	5 43	6 29	9 1	....	....	....	....	....

Miles	Up.	mrn	mrn	mrn	non (Commences on 17th inst.)	aft	aft	aft	aft					
	Newquay .... dep.	7 15	8 50	11 5	12 0	1252	1 50	5 15	7 30	....	....	....	....	....
2¾	Quintrel Downs Platform	....	8 58	1112	....	1259	1 58	5 23	7 38	....	....	....	....	....
6½	St. Columb Road ‡	7 30	9 8	1122	1216	1 11	2 7	5 32	7 48	....	....	....	....	....
2	Roche	7 44	9 25	1136	....	1 27	....	5 46	8 2	....	....	....	....	....
4½	Bugle	7 51	9 32	1143	....	1 34	....	6 5	8 9	....	....	....	....	....
6½	Luxulyan	7 59	9 39	1150	....	1 40	....	6 11	8 17	....	....	....	....	....
0¼	St. Blazey	8 15	9 50	12 3	1247	1 52	....	6 22	8 39	....	....	....	....	....
0¾	Par 20, 24 .... arr.	8 17	9 52	12 5	1249	1 54	2 40	6 25	8 41	....	....	....	....	....

NOTES.

n Stop to set down from London on informing the Guard at Par.

† Station for St. Columb Minor (2 miles); also for Watergate Bay.

‡ Station for St. Columb Major (2¼ miles).

1922

Miles	Down.	mrn	mrn	aft	aft	aft	aft	aft
	Truro .... dep.	7 40	9g25	12g7	2 55	2g22	4g25	8g5
5¼	Chacewater .... arr.	7 52	9g37	12g20	3 7	2g25	4g38	8g17
–	27 PENZANCE .... dep.	....	9 10	10 30		1 55	....	7 15
–	Chacewater ¶ .... dep.	7 53	10 12	12 25	Weds. & Sats.	3 10	4 45	8 20
8½	St. Agnes	8 3	10 22	12 35		3 20	4 56	8 30
3¾	Perranporth	8 17	10 36	12 49		3 34	5 10	8 44
7¾	Shepherds	8 33	10 52	1 5		3 50	5 26	9 0
3¾	Newquay ¶ *(below)* .... arr.	8 49	11 8	1 21		4 6	5 42	9 16

Miles	Up.	mrn	mrn	mrn	aft	aft	aft	aft
	Newquay ¶ .... dep.	7 45	9 0	11 12	1 30	Weds. & Sats.	4 35	6 10
6	Shepherds	8 5	9 20	11 32	1 50		4 55	6 29
10¼	Perranporth	8 18	9 33	11 45	2 8		5 10	6 43
15¼	St. Agnes	8 34	9 49	12 1	2 19		5 26	6 58
18½	Chacewater ¶ 22 .... arr.	8 45	10 0	12 12	2 30		5 37	7 9
39	22 PENZANCE .... arr.	....	11 32	1 20	3 35		7 55	8 20
—	Chacewater .... dep.	9g7	10 1	1g10	3g0	2 38	5 45	7 10
23¾	Truro 22, 27 .... arr.	9g17	10 11	1g20	3g10	2 50	5 57	7 22

g By Train, 1st and 3rd class. ¶ "Halts" at Mount Hawke, between Chacewater and St. Agnes; Goonbell and Mithian, between St. Agnes and Perranporth; Goonhavern, between Perranporth and Shepherds; and Mitchell and Newlyn and Trewerry and Trerice, between Shepherds and Newquay.

☞ For **OTHER TRAINS** between Truro and Chacewater, see page 22.

PAR, ST. BLAZEY, and NEWQUAY.—Great Western.

Down.	mrn	mrn	mrn	mrn	aft	aft	aft	aft	
Par .... dep.	6 5	....	9 25	11 5	1230	2 25	4 25	6 25	...
St. Blazey	6 10	....	9 30	11 9	1235	2 29	4 29	6 29	...
Luxulyan	6 23	....	9 44	1121	1250	2 43	....	6 41	...
Bugle	6 32	....	9 49	1127	1257	2 50	....	6 47	...
Roche	6 42	....	9 57	1134	1 6	2 58	4 52	6 54	...
St. Columb Road §	7 5	8 25	1010	1148	1 31	3 14	5 6	7 8	...
Quintrel Downs Plat.	....	8 35	1020	1158	1 45	3 24	....	7 18	...
Newquay ‡ *(above)*. arr.	7 25	8 43	1028	12 6	1 55	3 32	5 18	7 26	...

Miles	Up.	mrn	mrn	aft	aft	aft	aft	
	Newquay .... dep.	8 55	1115	1235	2 50	4 50	6 20	....
2½	Quintrel Downs Plat.	9 3	1122	1242	2 57	4 57	6 27	....
6½	St. Columb Road §	9 13	1132	1252	3 12	5 7	6 37	....
12	Roche	9 30	1147	1 7	3 26	5 22	6 55	....
14¼	Bugle	9 37	1154	1 14	3 32	5 29	7 2	....
16¼	Luxulyan	9 45	12 0	1 20	3 39	5 35	7 8	....
20¼	St. Blazey	9 57	1213	1 32	3 50	5 47	7 20	....
20¾	Par 22, 27, *below* .. arr.	9 59	1215	1 34	3 52	5 50	7 22	....

‡ Station for St. Columb Minor (2 miles); also for Watergate Bay. § Station for St. Columb Major (2¼ miles).

1938

Down.	mrn	mrn	mrn	mrn	S		aft	aft	aft		aft	aft	Sundays			
Truro .... dep.	..	7 26	8B19	9B5	11 25	..	1 5	3 10	4 35	..	6 0	8B30	..	..	..	..
Chacewater ¶	6 30	7 37	8 35	10 7	11 36	..	1 16	3 21	4 46	..	6 11	8 43	..	..	..	..
St. Agnes	6 40	7 47	8 45	1017	11 46	..	1 27	3 31	4 55	..	6 21	8 53	..	..	..	..
Perranporth	6 55	8 4	9 0	1033	12 3	..	1 45	3 46	5 13	..	6 37	9 10	..	..	..	..
Shepherds	7 10	8 19	..	1048	12 18	..	2 2	4 0	5 28	..	6 52	9 25	..	..	..	..
Newquay ¶ *(below)* .. arr.	7 25	8 34	..	11 3	12 33	..	2 18	4 16	5 43	..	7 7	9 40	..	..	..	..

Up.	mrn	mrn	mrn	mrn		S	aft	aft	aft	aft			Sundays			
Newquay ¶ .... dep.	7 34	..	8 52	11 30	..	1240	1 45	4 44	6 5	7 20	..	..	..	..	..	..
Shepherds	7 52	..	9 10	11 48	..	1258	2 3	5 2	6 23	7 38	..	..	..	..	..	..
Perranporth	8 2	9 4	9 22	12 1	..	1 11	2 16	5 14	6 36	7 50	..	..	..	..	..	..
St. Agnes	8 19	9 20	9 39	12 18	..	1 28	2 33	5 31	6 53	8 7	..	..	..	..	..	..
Chacewater ¶ 26	8 28	9 30	9 48	12 27	..	1 37	2 42	5 40	7 2	8 16	..	..	..	..	..	..
Truro 26, 31, 63 ... arr.	8B43	9B43	10B0	12 37	..	1 47	2 52	6B0	7 12	8B28	..	..	..	..	..	..

¶ "Halts" at Mount Hawke, between Chacewater and St. Agnes; at Goonbell, at Mithian, and at Perranporth Beach, between St. Agnes and Perranporth; at Goonhavern, between Perranporth and Shepherds; at Mitchell and Newlyn and at Trewerry and Trerice, between Shepherds and Newquay.

B Change at Chacewater E Except Sats S Sats only

OTHER TRAINS between Truro & Chacewater, page 26

PAR, BUGLE, and NEWQUAY.

Down.	mrn		mrn		mrn		mrn		aft	aft		aft		aft		S	Sundays						
Par .... dep.	6 30	..	7 35	..	9 10	..	1018	..	12 5	2 22	..	3 45	..	6 12	..	9 30	..	..	..	..	..	..	..
Luxulyan	6 45	..	7 49	..	9 25	..	1034	..	1225	2 39	..	3 59	..	6 28	..	9 44	..	..	..	..	..	..	..
Bugle	6 51	..	7 55	..	9 30	..	1038	..	1232	2 44	..	4 5	..	6 35	..	9 49	..	..	..	..	..	..	..
Roche	6 58	..	8 2	..	9 33	..	..	..	1239	2 50	..	4 11	..	6 40	..	9 55	..	..	..	..	..	..	..
St. Columb Road **A**	7 15	..	8 15	..	9 50	..	1057	..	1255	3 4	..	4 23	..	6 54	..	1010	..	..	..	..	..	..	..
Quintrel Downs Plat. ...	..	..	8 24	..	10 0	..	..	..	1 4	3 13	..	4 32	..	7 2	..	..	..	..	..	..	..	..	..
Newquay **B** *(above)* arr.	7 27	..	8 30	..	10 8	..	1110	..	1 15	3 20	..	4 40	..	7 10	..	1025	..	..	..	..	..	..	..

Up.	mrn		mrn		mrn		aft	aft		aft	aft		aft		aft	Sundays						
Newquay .... dep.	8 45	..	1030	..	1115	..	1240	2 35	..	4 47	6 10	..	8 15	..	9 55	..	..	..	..	..	..	..
Quintrel Downs Plat. ...	8 50	..	..	..	1121	..	1245	2 41	..	4 53	6 16	..	8 21	..	10 1	..	..	..	..	..	..	..
St. Columb Road **A**	9 0	..	1044	..	1131	..	1255	2 51	..	5 2	6 26	..	8 31	..	10 11	..	..	..	..	..	..	..
Roche	9 14	..	..	..	1145	..	1 10	3 5	..	5 16	6 41	..	8 45	..	10 25	..	..	..	..	..	..	..
Bugle	9 20	..	..	..	1151	..	1 16	3 11	..	5 22	6 47	..	8 51	..	10 31	..	..	..	..	..	..	..
Luxulyan	9 26	..	..	..	1157	..	1 22	3 17	..	5 28	6 53	..	8 57	..	10 37	..	..	..	..	..	..	..
Par 26, 31 .... arr.	9 39	..	1120	..	1212	..	1 36	3 35	..	5 40	7 6	..	9 9	..	10 49	..	..	..	..	..	..	..

A Station for St. Columb Major (2¼ miles). **B** Station for St. Columb Minor (2 miles); also for Watergate Bay.
E Except Sats. **S** Sats. only.

1. From Par

PAR

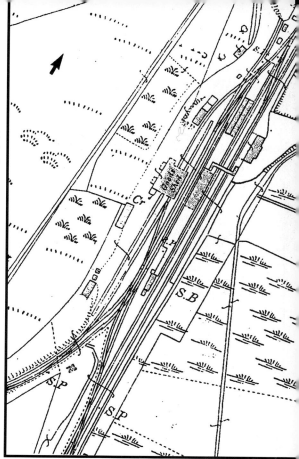

IV.   The 1907 map shows a track layout that was little changed for the subsequent 50 years or more. The main line runs diagonally and the "Par Loop" to St. Blazey is on the left.

Other views of this station can be found in our *Plymouth to St. Austell* album - pictures 105 to 113.

1.   A goods train stands at the up platform; Newquay branch trains would wait to the right of the footbridge. The fence was removed in 1913 to allow the platform to be altered as shown in the next picture. The roof on the right is over a coal store, which is adjacent to the cattle pens. (M.Dart coll.)

2.　　A 1922 view features a 3581 class 2-4-0T running round the branch train, while a single coach stands at the down platform, probably having been detached from an express. The 6.25pm to Newquay at this time similarly detached a portion for Fowey when it reached St. Blazey, which is in the right background. (LGRP/NRM)

3.　　The goods shed originally had tracks of different gauges and was mainly used for transhipment purposes. It was partly used for carriage storage until 1965. We witness the arrival of the 7.50am Newquay to Manchester, where the train was due at 7.24pm. No. 4167 is piloting no. 6869 *Resolven Grange* on 9th July 1955. (R.C.Riley / Transport Treasury)

4. The 2-6-2T is seen again, but this time on a stopping train to Newquay on 22nd August 1956. The goods shed was to remain in use until 1st October 1964, but the gas lighting was soon to cease. There was a small buffet on this platform. (N.L.Browne)

5. Electric lights would make life easier for locomotive crews watering at night. 0-6-0PT no. 4673 is being refreshed on 4th July 1961 after arrival from Newquay. This view is included to show the goods yard access. (M.Dart)

6.   A Derby-built suburban service 3-car class 116 DMU waits to form the 15.45 to Newquay on 15th June 1967. The wagon in the background stands on the goods shed siding. Both shed and siding were removed the following year to make room for a freightliner container handling facility. Unfortunately regular freightliner workings to Devon and Cornwall never materialised and the new investment saw little use. (G.Gillham)

7.   A two-car DMU arrives from Newquay on 10th August 1976 and approaches the 57-lever signal box, which was built in 1890. It had a panel added in 1965 to control parts of the main line, but traditional signalling was still in use locally in 2001. (M.Turvey)

8.   A train of loaded "clay hoods" rounds the double track curve from St. Blazey on 30th March 1984, destined for Carne Point near Fowey, via Lostwithiel. On the left, an HST climbs towards the bridge which crosses the line to Par Harbour and which also spanned the branch to Fowey until 1968. New premises for the signal engineers are under construction on the right. (P.G.Barnes)

9.   "Skipper" no. 142027 has just used the crossover on 1st May 1987 as it approaches the platform, which has a track signalled for bidirectional running. These railcars were unsuccessful on the branches of Devon and Cornwall, soon being sent elsewhere. (P.G.Barnes)

10. Three more semaphore signals are visible as the evening sun illuminates the last train of the day to Newquay (the 18.00) on 24th April 1989. The waiting room can be seen; this was provided after the original buildings had been demolished. (G.Gillham)

11. A class 158 DMU waits at the up platform on 23rd May 1998 for the Paddington to Newquay HST to cross to the branch, which had received this type of stock since May 1988, but on Summer Saturdays and Sundays only. However, they were absent for two years following a derailment south of Luxulyan Tunnel on 25th May 1991. (M.J.Stretton)

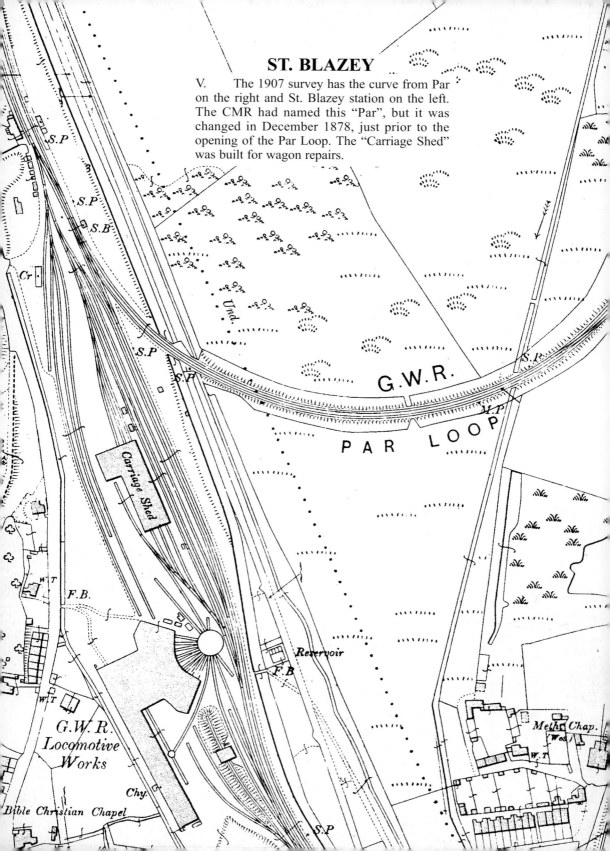

ST. BLAZEY

V.   The 1907 survey has the curve from Par on the right and St. Blazey station on the left. The CMR had named this "Par", but it was changed in December 1878, just prior to the opening of the Par Loop. The "Carriage Shed" was built for wagon repairs.

S.P.

S.P.

S.B.

Cr.

Und.

S.P.

S.P.

Carriage Shed

G.W.R.

S.P.

M.P.

PAR LOOP

W.T.

F.B.

Reservoir

F.B.

W.T.

Meth. Chap.
(Wes)

W.T.

G.W.R.
Locomotive
Works

Chy.

Bible Christian Chapel

S.P.

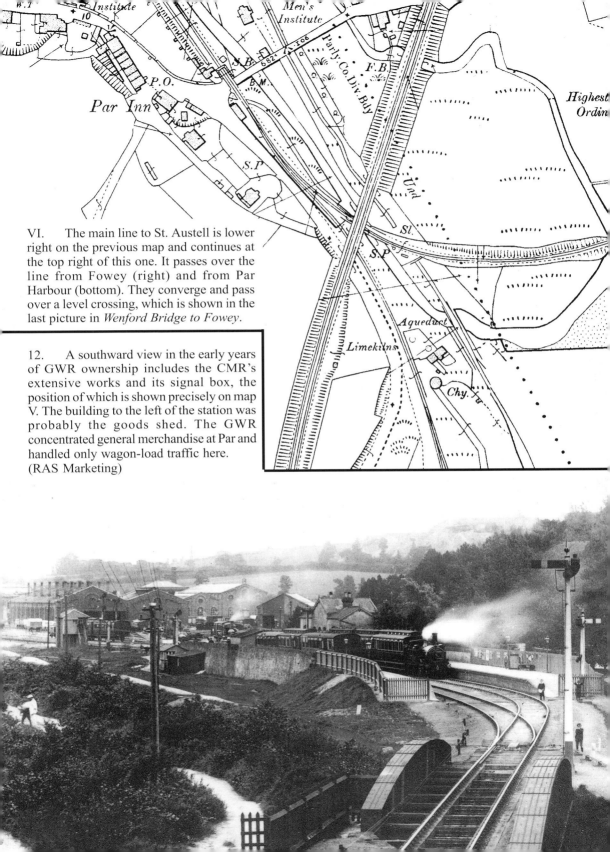

VI.   The main line to St. Austell is lower right on the previous map and continues at the top right of this one. It passes over the line from Fowey (right) and from Par Harbour (bottom). They converge and pass over a level crossing, which is shown in the last picture in *Wenford Bridge to Fowey.*

12.   A southward view in the early years of GWR ownership includes the CMR's extensive works and its signal box, the position of which is shown precisely on map V. The building to the left of the station was probably the goods shed. The GWR concentrated general merchandise at Par and handled only wagon-load traffic here. (RAS Marketing)

13.   We now have two views recorded from the footbridge in 1922. On the left are the remains of the CMR signal box and the curve to Par, while in the centre is a freight train arriving from the north. It is on a goods loop that was laid behind the station building in about 1910. It is probably the rear of this train that appears near the fence in the next picture. (LGRP/NRM)

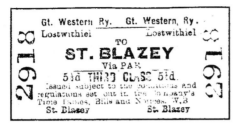

14.   The sidings on the left also date from about 1910, as did the footbridge which spanned their approach and linked the platforms. The station was closed to ordinary passengers on 29th September 1925, but was used by workmen employed at Fowey until 31st December 1934. Part of the footbridge was re-erected at St. Austell in 1931 and is still in use at the west end of the station. (LGRP/NRM)

CORNWALL MINERALS RAILWAY.

PAR   **PAR**   PAR

TO

FOWEY **FOWEY** FOWEY

THIRD CLASS.

By Ordinary Train.

This Ticket is issued subject to the conditions set forth in the Company's Time Tables for the present Month.

9297

St. Blazey	1903	1913	1923	1933
Passenger tickets issued	15972	21162	21910	Closed for Passenger Traffic Sept 1925
Season tickets issued	*	*	225	
Parcels forwarded	941	1013	462	
Coal and coke received (tons)	9618	9498	447	1743
General goods forwarded (tons)	364	2620	1619	988
Other minerals received (tons)	24645	37568	20427	25707
General goods received (tons)	72	873	546	951
Trucks of livestock handled	-	-	-	-
(* not available. Seasons include holiday Runabouts.)				

15.   The GWR erected one of its standard combined water tank/coal stage structures in 1896. The wagon on the left contained loco coal, which was shovelled out onto a steel deck or into tubs prior to transfer to bunkers. To the left of the ash handling crane on 26th September 1956 is no. 5193, while no. 4247 arrives with more china clay bound for Fowey. (H.C.Casserley)

16.   The CMR built a semi-roundhouse in which to house its fleet of 18 0-6-0Ts ordered from Sharp Stewart, but only about half of them were used owing to the economic conditions. Beyond the turntable, no. 4585 is being lifted for repairs. The building has a Grade II listing status. (H.C.Casserley)

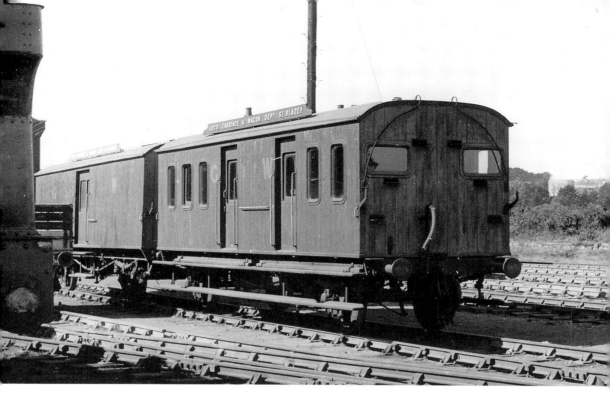

17.	The depot had its own tool van and mess coach for its breakdown gang. Around 35 locomotives were allocated to the shed (numbered 83E) in the mid-1950s. The entire staff of the CMR numbered 39 when it opened; there were 53 at St. Blazey alone in 1923. (J.H.Aston)

18.	Steam traction on the branch ended in 1962. No. D816 is passing the locomotive shed on 12th July 1960, during the transitional period. Named *Eclipse,* this diesel was of the "Warship" class. (R.C.Riley / Transport Treasury)

19.   The GWR opened this signal box on 25th June 1908 and its 41-lever frame was still functioning nearly a century later. Electric train tokens were in use to Goonbarrow Junction. Photographed in July 1961, the CMR building was soon to be demolished. It was brick built, but the rendering had eliminated the corbels provided for a canopy that was probably never erected. (R.C.Riley / Transport Treasury)

20.   A single railcar is coupled to a 3-car DMU and is proceeding to Par on 12th September 1973 as no. D1000 reverses with empties from Fowey. No. D4161 is shunting loaded clay wagons. A traction maintenance depot was established here on 30th April 1987 and two years later there were eleven class 37s and one 08 based here. (D.H.Mitchell)

21.   Seen on the same day is class 25 no. 7625 and in the background is part of the workshops. All the CMR structures were built of Devonshire bricks, an unusual procedure in those days. The engine shed was leased out for commercial purposes after its closure in April 1987. The turntable was vacuum operated; hence the large cylinders and a hose for connection to the locomotive. It was still usable in 2001. (D.H.Mitchell)

22.   Now we have four photographs from 2nd October 1997, this one being from the cab of a locomotive running on the curve from Par. The platform was being resurfaced mainly for the benefit of staff. It had been used by Newquay passengers on 19th April 1984, due to a derailment on the curve to Par. On the right is "Ballast Siding", which was once used for carriage berthing. (V.Mitchell)

23.   The wagon repair shop was recorded at 07.10 when work was in full swing. A large fleet of high capacity vehicles was maintained here, many of them never leaving Cornwall. The building is in the centre of picture 13. (V.Mitchell)

24.　This platform is completely out of public view on the west side of the site. It has an associated concrete apron and was intended for the washing of clay wagons, but there were problems with lack of adequate water pressure. It has however been used for servicing DMUs. (V.Mitchell)

25.　A parking space for wheelsets was provided at the south end of the site, as they were transported by road. One of the once extensive fleet of "clay hoods" had been preserved on a plinth by depot staff, after the last was withdrawn in February 1988. They were a great improvement on the type seen in pictures 13 and 14, which were prone to develop large heavy puddles on their sheets. (V.Mitchell)

26. Middleway Bridge Crossing once had a footbridge; this can be seen in the background of picture 14. We witness the passage of the 16.58 Newquay to Par, headed by no. 47035 on 18th June 1977, over clay dusted track. (T.Heavyside)

27. No. 08792 moved a massive silo from Pontsmill to Par Harbour on 1st February 1995. It was greatly out of gauge and so the bracket signals had been rotated through 90 degrees. There was a seven-lever signal box to the left of the view until 30th August 1981 when full lifting barriers came into use. The rods and wires pass over the river in the previous picture. (M.Dart coll.)

28.   This box was half a mile to the north and had five levers. It had been moved here from Morlais Junction in 1913 and controlled gates on the A390 until full lifting barriers were installed on 30th September 1972. The barriers at both crossings were worked from St. Blazey under CCTV. (G.Gillham)

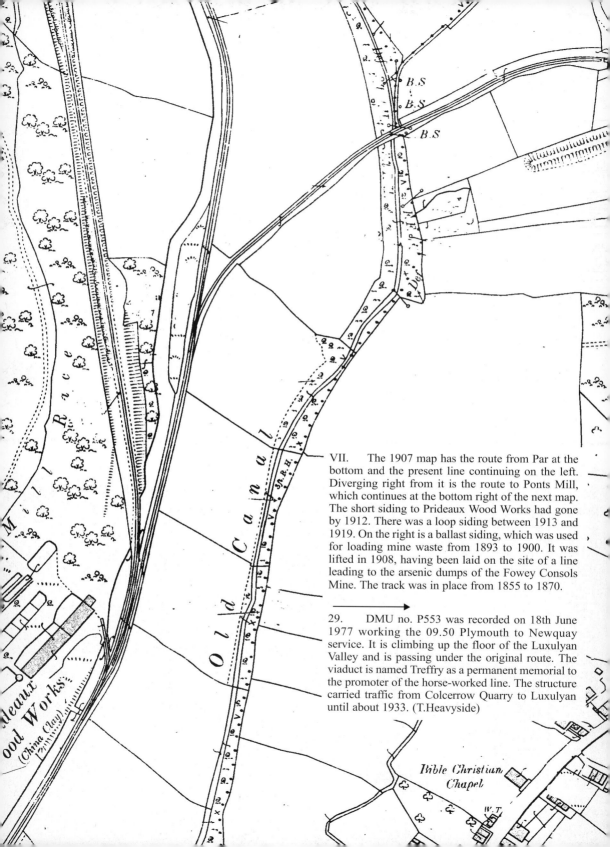

VII.   The 1907 map has the route from Par at the bottom and the present line continuing on the left. Diverging right from it is the route to Ponts Mill, which continues at the bottom right of the next map. The short siding to Prideaux Wood Works had gone by 1912. There was a loop siding between 1913 and 1919. On the right is a ballast siding, which was used for loading mine waste from 1893 to 1900. It was lifted in 1908, having been laid on the site of a line leading to the arsenic dumps of the Fowey Consols Mine. The track was in place from 1855 to 1870.

→

29.   DMU no. P553 was recorded on 18th June 1977 working the 09.50 Plymouth to Newquay service. It is climbing up the floor of the Luxulyan Valley and is passing under the original route. The viaduct is named Treffry as a permanent memorial to the promoter of the horse-worked line. The structure carried traffic from Colcerrow Quarry to Luxulyan until about 1933. (T.Heavyside)

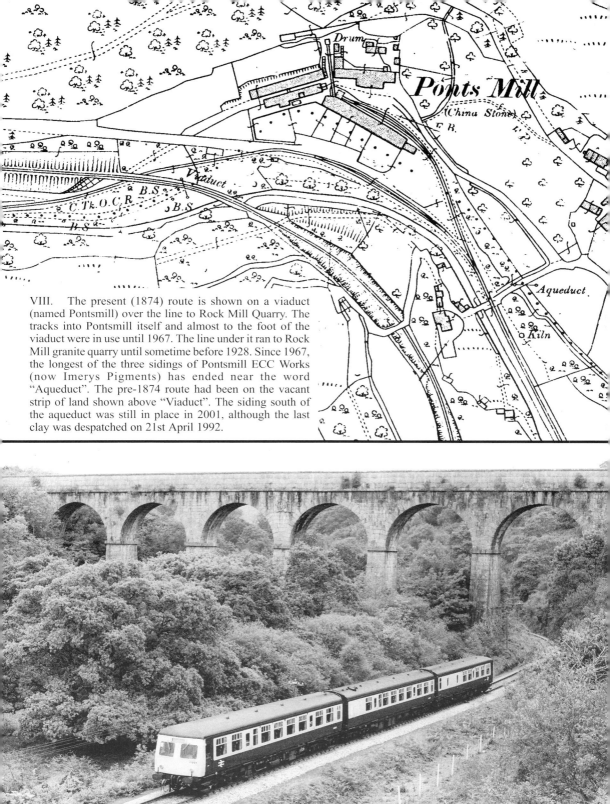

VIII.   The present (1874) route is shown on a viaduct (named Pontsmill) over the line to Rock Mill Quarry. The tracks into Pontsmill itself and almost to the foot of the viaduct were in use until 1967. The line under it ran to Rock Mill granite quarry until sometime before 1928. Since 1967, the longest of the three sidings of Pontsmill ECC Works (now Imerys Pigments) has ended near the word "Aqueduct". The pre-1874 route had been on the vacant strip of land shown above "Viaduct". The siding south of the aqueduct was still in place in 2001, although the last clay was despatched on 21st April 1992.

30.   The 9.30am Paddington to Newquay was loaded to 12 coaches on Saturday 9th July 1955; the weight being in excess of 500 tons, three locomotives were required on the 1 in 39 gradient. They are nos 5972 *Olton Hall*, 6397 and at the rear is 2-6-2T no. 5519. A "Hall" was only allowed 190 tons unassisted. (R.C.Riley / Transport Treasury)

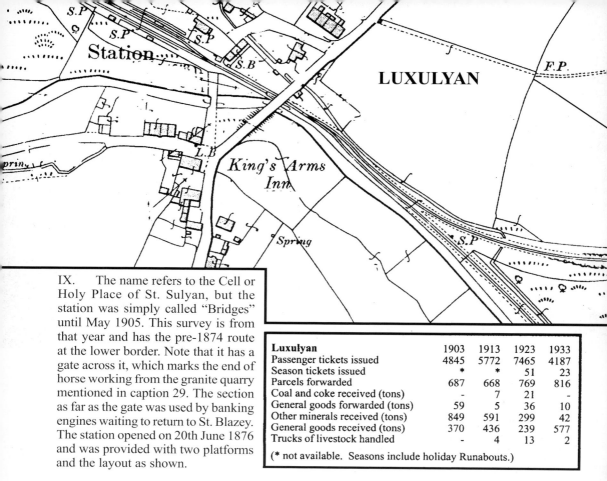

LUXULYAN

IX.   The name refers to the Cell or Holy Place of St. Sulyan, but the station was simply called "Bridges" until May 1905. This survey is from that year and has the pre-1874 route at the lower border. Note that it has a gate across it, which marks the end of horse working from the granite quarry mentioned in caption 29. The section as far as the gate was used by banking engines waiting to return to St. Blazey. The station opened on 20th June 1876 and was provided with two platforms and the layout as shown.

Luxulyan	1903	1913	1923	1933
Passenger tickets issued	4845	5772	7465	4187
Season tickets issued	*	*	51	23
Parcels forwarded	687	668	769	816
Coal and coke received (tons)	-	7	21	-
General goods forwarded (tons)	59	5	36	10
Other minerals received (tons)	849	591	299	42
General goods received (tons)	370	436	239	577
Trucks of livestock handled	-	4	13	2

(* not available. Seasons include holiday Runabouts.)

31.   The loop was lengthened greatly and an island platform was built in 1910. A new signal box (illustrated) came into use on 30th March 1911. The wind pump supplied locomotive water. The wharf in the yard was once used for transfer of china clay from a horse-worked narrow gauge line. (LGRP/NRM)

32.   The 5.8pm Par to Newquay runs into the island platform on 16th August 1959, hauled by no. 4906 *Bradfield Hall*. The station building is the squat one on the left and was of CMR origin. (P.Hay)

33.   Camping coaches were positioned behind the smoke in the next picture in 1936-39 and again in 1952-63. This view is from July 1960 and is of no. W9906W. There was a staff of 3 or 4 men between 1903 and 1938, but manning ceased on 12th July 1964. (M.H.Walshaw)

34.　　No. 1664 leaves with the Goonbarrow branch goods on 13th July 1961. On the right is Treskilling Clay Works, which had its own siding between about 1916 and 1964. The box had 27 levers. (P.W.Gray)

35.　　The goods yard and signal box had closed on 27th September 1964 and the site had become overgrown by the time that the 09.40 from Par was photographed on 29th September 1978. The Pagoda shelter was replaced by a plain hut a few years later. (D.H.Mitchell)

GOONBARROW JUNCTION

X.   The single line from Luxulyan is the upper one on the right, the others being sidings. Although this map is from 1906, the basic plan has not changed greatly to this day. The main change was that the route was doubled westward in July 1930. This became two parallel single tracks in November 1964. On the left is the Wheal Henry siding and the Goonbarrow branch which served eight different clay producers. The lines at the bottom eventually served four such firms. One was serving Imery's Rock Dryers as the 21st century began.

Goonbarrow
Junction

36.   No. 5521 has just entered the double track section with a passenger train from Par, while no. 5519 waits with a pilot engine to enter the single line, in June 1958. The vans are standing on the up refuge siding. Around 500,000 tonnes of clay per annum were despatched in the 1990s. (N.Simmons)

37.   The 25-lever box opened in 1909; its predecessor was called Rosvear Siding until 1893. After exchanging tokens with the signalman on 27th April 1989, the driver of class 122 "Bubble Car" no. M55009 accelerates away towards Newquay with the 14.40 from Par. Goonbarrow is now the northern limit of china clay working on the branch and also the only surviving passing loop. M55009 had recently been transferred from Tyseley, hence the "West Midland Lines" logo on the side. (G.Gillham)

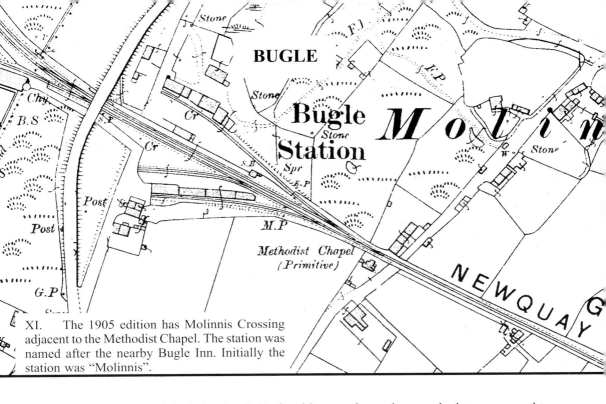

XI.   The 1905 edition has Molinnis Crossing adjacent to the Methodist Chapel. The station was named after the nearby Bugle Inn. Initially the station was "Molinnis".

38.   A 1906 photograph includes the CMR signal box, station and crane; the latter was used to load half-ton casks of china clay. (M.Dart coll.)

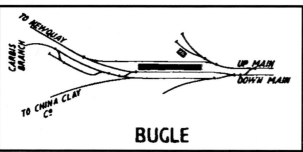

BUGLE

39.   This 1922 view includes the iron clad shed that was added for parcels traffic. Note the improved crane. The left bridge span was over roadway to the hamlet of Hallew. (LGRP/NRM)

XII.   The 1933 diagram shows the island platform that came into use on 20th July 1930 and the branch to Wheal Rose, lower left.

BUGLE STEAM RAILWAY

Established in 1976, the rolling stock included ex- Devonport Dockyard Bagnall 0-4-0ST no.19, Peckett 0-4-0ST *Progress,* a Peckett 0-4-0 fireless locomotive from Marsh Mills dries and an ex-GWR bogie coach of 1910. Most of the collection was moved to the expanding Bodmin & Wenford Railway in 1987.

Bugle	1903	1913	1923	1933
Passenger tickets issued	6293	8679	11725	11273
Season tickets issued	*	*	634	200
Parcels forwarded	1444	3779	3982	4483
Coal and coke received (tons)	-	106	187	-
General goods forwarded (tons)	93	257	355	317
Other minerals received (tons)	646	1335	2533	191
General goods received (tons)	2308	5684	3835	1845
Trucks of livestock handled	-	-	-	17
(* not available. Seasons include holiday Runabouts.)				

40.   No. 4906 *Bradfield Hall* is arriving with the 1.45pm Newquay to Par on 16th August 1959 and is passing under the additional span that was necessary for the doubling. The gate on the left is over the Wheal Rose branch, which was laid partly on the route of Treffry's Tramway to Molinnis. (P.Hay)

41.   The passenger line was singled on 29th November 1964 and the 41-lever signal box in the background was reduced to a ground frame. It was closed on 17th August 1973. Twelve men had been employed at this station for most of the 1930s. (Lens of Sutton)

42.   The 10.34 from Newquay has stopped on 29th September 1978 by which time Molinnis Crossing simply had lights activated by passenger trains. Mineral trains using the track on the right to Carbis had to stop at the board. The remaining building vanished around 1990. (D.H.Mitchell)

43.   The same train is seen a minute or so earlier, as it approaches the road bridge. The gate on the left is the one seen in picture 40; the nearby track ran to Carbis Wharf. To the right of this had been the former down line. It had joined the up line in the background until 1964. (D.H.Mitchell)

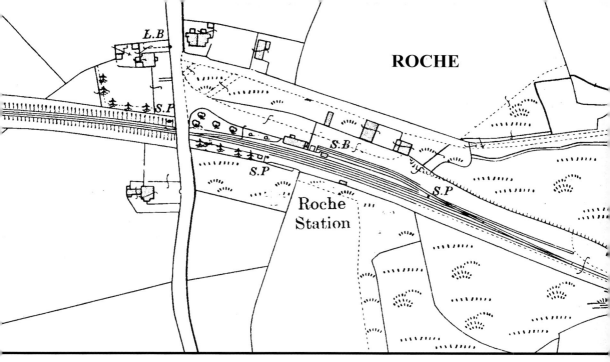

ROCHE

XIII.   The station was named "Victoria", after a nearby inn, until 1st May 1904. The village centre is about one mile to the south, but the name "Holywell" was used until 1879. This is the 1905 map; an extra siding was provided in 1920 and the loop was lengthened in 1936.

44.   This 1922 westward view includes a GWR perforated concrete signal post. There was a staff of five at this time and during most of the 1930s. (LGRP/NRM)

45.   This 1956 view features the CMR building and the GWR parcels shed and signal box. The latter was in use until 30th January 1965 and had a 24-lever frame. Unlike most of the other small stations, electric light was provided here. (H.C.Casserley)

46.   Both of the sidings are visible as the 11.0am from Newquay waits to depart for Par on 16th August 1959. The goods yard accommodated a camping coach in the Summer of 1963 only. (P.Hay)

Roche	1903	1913	1923	1933
Passenger tickets issued	4552	6238	6335	4818
Season tickets issued	*	*	196	127
Parcels forwarded	2492	3150	4501	3271
Coal and coke received (tons)	-	-	17	-
General goods forwarded (tons)	92	179	182	71
Other minerals received (tons)	197	150	1479	601
General goods received (tons)	591	1490	1918	1071
Trucks of livestock handled	79	12	38	29
(* not available. Seasons include holiday Runabouts.)				

47.   Staffing ceased on 13th July 1964, the goods yard having closed on 1st June of that year. The down platform was retained, although it was the up one that was used for the first six months after the signal box closure. (Lens of Sutton)

WEST OF ROCHE

48.	The bridge over the A30 had been wooden and was replaced with a steel structure in 1930. It was at the summit of the route, as can be seen by the vertical bend in this southbound clay train in 1957. The guard is obeying the order on the board to pin down brakes for the descent. The locomotives are 2-8-0T no. 4294 and a 2-6-2T of class 4575. (D.Lawrence)

49.	The wide expanse of Goss Moor is evident. Having crossed the bowstring bridge over the busy A30, no. 37267 heads a train of loaded clay hoods from Meledor Mill to Fowey on 29th June 1979. Because this bridge restricts any road widening, it has been suggested that Newquay trains run from St. Austell via Burngullow to St. Dennis Junction enabling the existing Goonbarrow to St. Dennis Junction route to be abandoned. Subsequent plans envisage diverting the road east of the railway. The triangle on the bridge warns of another problem - a height restriction of 14ft 3ins. (G.Gillham)

50.   The line runs parallel to the A30 across Goss Moor for about three miles. A turning south from it, about mid-way, necessitated a level crossing. The signal box was called Tregoss Moor and the first one opened in 1914. This one was in use as a block post from 10th September 1921 until 3rd January 1965, during which period double track was provided from here to St. Dennis Junction. (M.Dart coll.)

51.   The eight-lever box controlled the crossing until an Automatic Open Crossing was provided on 25th May 1973. The 13.10 from Par on 1st August 1981 is making the regulation speed reduction as it approaches the former crossing keepers cottage. (D.H.Mitchell)

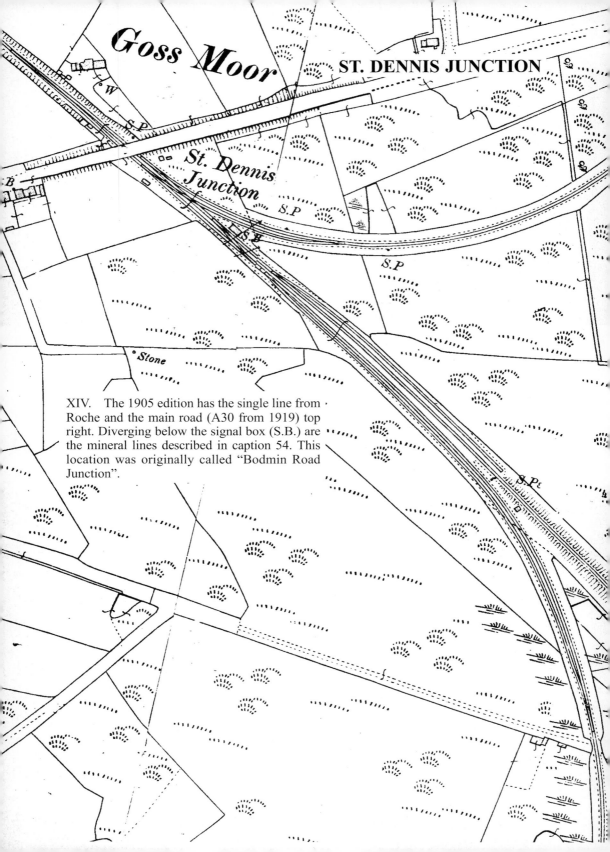

Goss Moor

ST. DENNIS JUNCTION

St. Dennis
Junction

Stone

XIV.   The 1905 edition has the single line from
Roche and the main road (A30 from 1919) top
right. Diverging below the signal box (S.B.) are
the mineral lines described in caption 54. This
location was originally called "Bodmin Road
Junction".

52.   The double track from Tregoss Moor is on the left in this 1922 panorama, which includes waste tips on the skyline. Left of centre is the GWR's own tip for rubbish and spent ballast. (LGRP/NRM)

53.   Viewed from the A30 bridge on 11th July 1955 is no. 4526 hauling a clay train off the mineral branch. Once clear of the points, the train will reverse and no. 4526 will act as a banker on the climb to Roche and be detached at Bugle. (R.C.Riley / Transport Treasury)

54.   The 11.44 from Par is subject to a 25mph speed limit on the curve and is seen on 29th September 1978. The other tracks diverge thus: left to the tip, centre to Drinnick Mill (and eventually Burngullow referred to in caption 49) and right to Meledor Mill. The signal box closed on 14th December 1986, the St. Dennis to Parkandillick section having been lost on 6th February 1966 and St. Dennis to Meledor Mill section following on 3rd April 1982. (D.H.Mitchell)

St.Columb Road	1903	1913	1923	1933
Passenger tickets issued	9341	15040	22201	14612
Season tickets issued	*	*	542	304
Parcels forwarded	8923	11732	20255	16757
Coal and coke received (tons)	-	-	28	18
General goods forwarded (tons)	524	691	600	568
Other minerals received (tons)	962	4005	672	954
General goods received (tons)	4033	4333	4065	3252
Trucks of livestock handled	205	278	328	153

(* not available. Seasons include holiday Runabouts.)

55.   This westward view was taken during shunting operations on 25th May 1922. Again we have the mixture of CMR and GWR buldings. There was a staff of 9 or 10 men here during the 1930s. (LGRP/NRM)

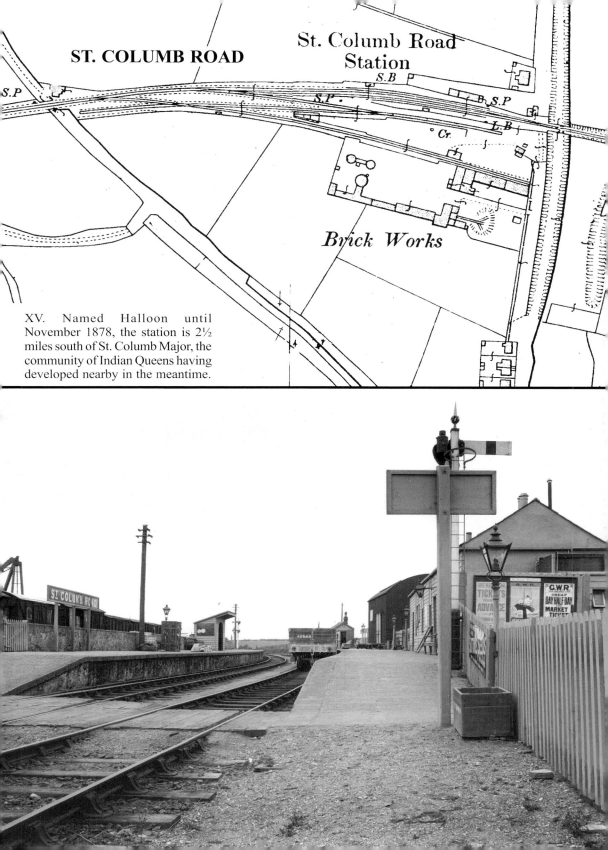

ST. COLUMB ROAD

St. Columb Road Station

Brick Works

XV. Named Halloon until November 1878, the station is 2½ miles south of St. Columb Major, the community of Indian Queens having developed nearby in the meantime.

56. The loop was extended in 1931-33, but abandoned on 3rd January 1965, when the signal box was closed. Goods traffic ceased on 7th September 1964, staff having been withdrawn on 12th July of that year. (Lens of Sutton)

QUINTREL DOWNS

XVI. The 1906 survey shows an arrangement that lasted until 1911, when the loop was removed and the signal box closed. Two extra sidings were laid: Shell-Mex and coal merchants Taylor & Low Bros. were using them in 1938.

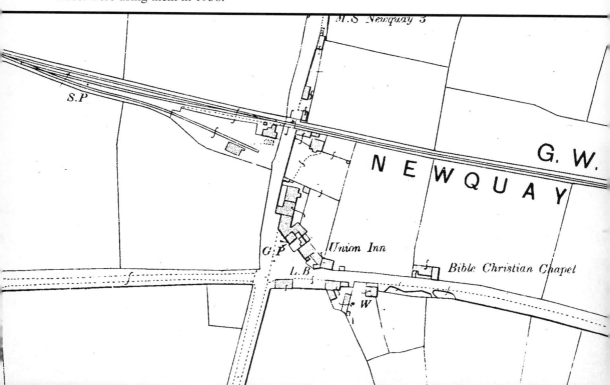

57.   A 1922 view from the level crossing reveals that a new platform was built on the site of the loop line and a siding was laid on the site of the old platform. The rod from the hut was for a gate lock. (LGRP/NRM)

58.   A June 1965 view includes one of the crossing gates on the A392. The goods yard closed on 7th September 1964. The suffix "Platform" was used until 1956. (R.M.Casserley)

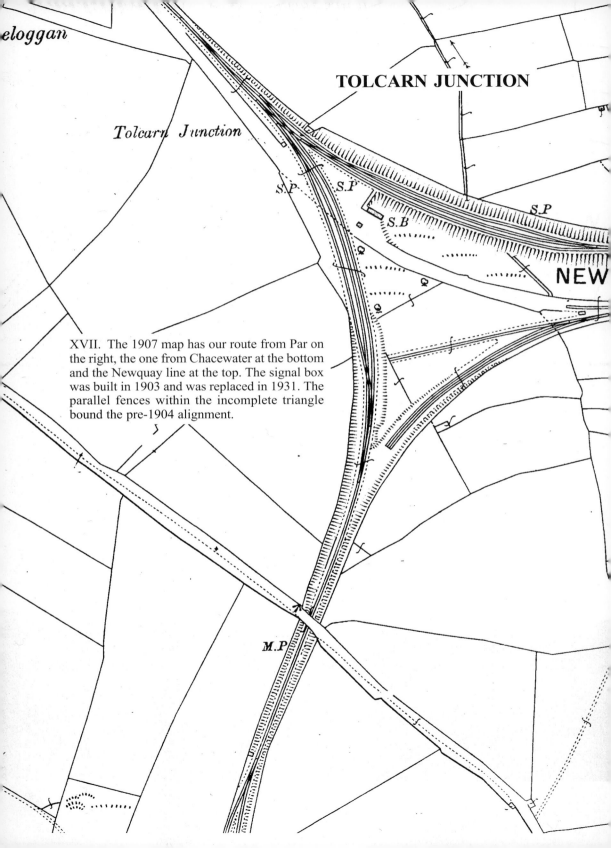

eloggan

TOLCARN JUNCTION

Tolcarn Junction

S.P   S.P   S.P

S.B

NEW

XVII. The 1907 map has our route from Par on the right, the one from Chacewater at the bottom and the Newquay line at the top. The signal box was built in 1903 and was replaced in 1931. The parallel fences within the incomplete triangle bound the pre-1904 alignment.

M.P

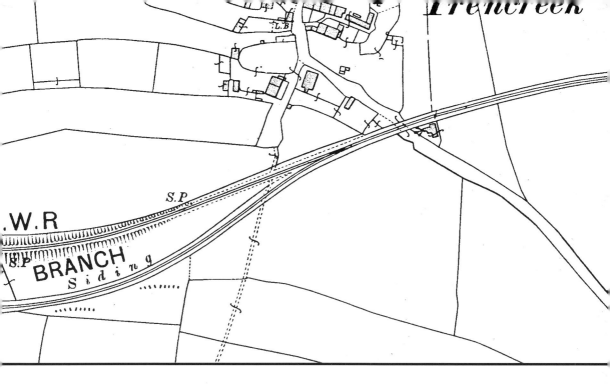

59.   Carriages stand in the sidings on the west side of the triangle. The Newquay line is in the distance and the route from Par is on the right. The track in the foreground of this 1948 photograph was used mainly for turning locomotives and never for regular passenger services. It came into use in 1931. The 52-lever Tolcarn Junction signal box (centre) was open from 20th July 1931 to 23rd November 1964. Most of the triangle is now covered with houses. (P.J.Garland/R.S.Carpenter coll.)

EAST OF NEWQUAY

60.   The 154yd-long Trenance Viaduct is at the approach to the station and was photographed in June 1921. This structure was completed by the CMR in 1873 and replaced by the GWR in 1938 by a double track multi-arch structure, although the two tracks did not come into use until 1946. The first viaduct was opened in 1849 and was a timber structure on granite piers. (K.Nunn/LCGB)

61.   Nearly-new class 142 "Skipper" unit no. 142026 has just crossed Trenance Viaduct and joins the single-line section to St. Dennis Junction forming the 13.30 service to Par on 24th April 1986. The short siding on the left is all that remained of the former double track to Tolcarn Junction - this had been singled when the junction signalbox closed in November 1964. (G.Gillham)

2. From Chacewater
CHACEWATER

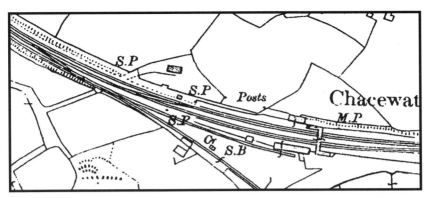

XVIII. The 1906 map reveals the layout before the loop was added for Newquay trains in 1912. The track westward, used by this service, was doubled in 1902. The route eastward followed in 1914.

Other views of this station can be found in pictures 35 to 40 in our *St. Austell to Penzance* album.

62.   A faded postcard includes the 1912 loop on the left. The station had only one platform until 1872. The signal box was in use from 1914 until 1977 and had 35 levers. The goods yard (right) closed on 5th October 1964 and was later converted to a cement distribution depot. This received rail traffic until 1987. (Lens of Sutton)

63.   A Newquay-bound train runs off the 128yd long Blackwater Viaduct in June 1956. The locomotive is 2-6-2T no. 4598 and the train includes an autocoach next to the brake van. (J.W.T.House/C.L.Caddy)

64.   A September 1956 view includes the new down side building which had been completed in the previous year. It replaced one destroyed by fire in 1947. (H.C.Casserley)

65.   No. 6828 *Trellech Grange* waits with an up train on 15th August 1959. The route to Newquay traverses the undulating terrain in the right background. (P.Hay)

66.   A Newquay train headed by 2-6-2T no. 5515 was recorded from a departing down train on 8th April 1960. The station was closed totally on 5th October 1964. (R.C.Riley / Transport Treasury)

BLACKWATER JUNCTION

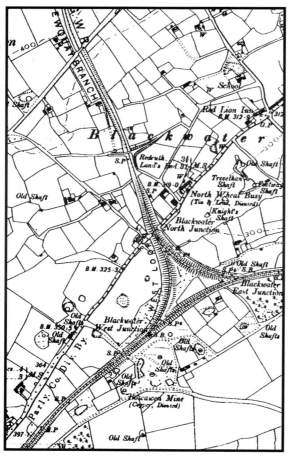

XIX.   The triangular junction was created in 1903 and is seen on the 1906 survey at 6ins to 1 mile. The main line is across the bottom and all three signal boxes are marked. The West Loop was little used and was taken out of use on 5th May 1919. All the signal boxes remained in use until 9th November 1924 when an independent third track from Chacewater came into use.

67.   This damaged snap is the only one known to show East Box. The line to Newquay curves under the front coach and North Box is in the background.
(C.Benney coll.)

70.   Construction details of the canopy show it to differ from the slightly later GWR design in which the truss spanned the entire building, eliminating the gulley. Note the shear legs used to aid bridge construction and also the light temporary way. (C.Benney coll.)

71.   The permanent way was to the usual high standard employed by the GWR, although traffic was light and steam railmotors of this type were generally used. There were four employees here initially, but three was the norm. (C.Benney coll.)

72.   Although from the same viewpoint, we include this picture as it unusually shows an autocoach attached to a railmotor. The former was intended for use with a tank engine. This one is being hauled; a rear lamp is visible. (C.Benney coll.)

73.   Here again an autocoach is not being used as intended, being sandwiched between the locomotive and an ordinary coach. The windswept treeless landscape is evident in the background. The goods shed was demolished in 1963, but the main building was in commercial use in 2001 and an ex-Devonport Dockyard four-wheeled diesel was standing near the road. (Lens of Sutton)

St. Agnes	1903	1913	1923	1933
Passenger tickets issued	-	17085	16073	9617
Season tickets issued	*	*	208	299
Parcels forwarded	8064	2622	4403	6231
Coal and coke received (tons)	-	8	-	-
General goods forwarded (tons)	160	270	211	126
Other minerals received (tons)	36	222	92	1230
General goods received (tons)	126	711	557	339
Trucks of livestock handled	16	50	23	46

(* not available. Seasons include holiday Runabouts.)

74.   A 1948 panorama shows the result of the alteration in 1937, when an island platform, a footbridge and a signal box were provided. The building lost its canopy and the doorways thereunder. The signal box had 30 levers. (P.J.Garland/R.S.Carpenter coll.)

75.   Camping coaches were present in the Summers of 1934-39 and 1952-63, the number ranging from one to three. The goods yard closed with the station and signal box on 4th February 1963, but the footbridge had vanished earlier. (Lens of Sutton)

76.   Farmer W.G.Bradley loaded all his equipment, plus 90 head of Ayrshire cattle, on 31st October 1958 and moved to a new farm near Raglan in Monmouthshire. (K.Young)

77.   The driver of no. 5562 saw the guard's green flag, but failed to check the signal. The catch points are seen more clearly in picture 74. The vans examined in picture 17 are on the left, as a tender engine (unusual on this route) tows the victim backwards in the rain. (K.Young)

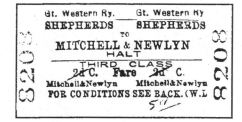

GOONBELL HALT

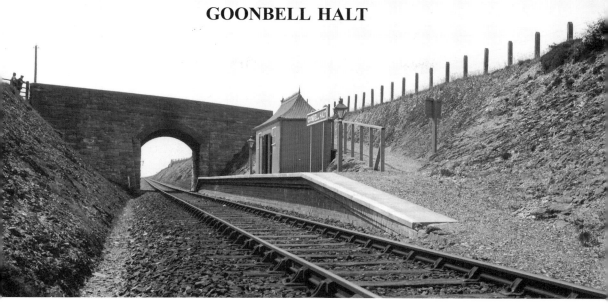

78.   This and the next halt are both shown on map XX and both were opened on 14th August 1905, more than two years after the line, at the time of the introduction of railmotors. (LGRP/NRM)

79.   A 1959 view shows the halt beyond the bridge. Its short length required the driver to stop the middle coach, containing the guard and hopefully any passengers, at the platform. (P.Hay)

MITHIAN HALT

80. A local photographer recorded this important addition to local transport. The resultant post-card would be sent far and wide as a news item. (C.Benney coll.)

81. By 1922 the GWR had regarded the halt as a success and replaced the timber platform, but not the fencing. Unusually, this halt was close to the village it served. (LGRP/NRM)

PERRANPORTH BEACH HALT

82.   This halt opened later than all the others, on 20th July 1931. It served not only holidaymakers, but local residents, as evidenced by the shoppers striding away from the train in September 1956. (N.L.Browne)

83.   Other unusual aspects of this halt were electric lighting and platform length. Some Summer trains called at this halt but not at the others. The gradient is 1 in 45 towards the sea, which is behind the camera. (M.Dart coll.)

PERRANPORTH

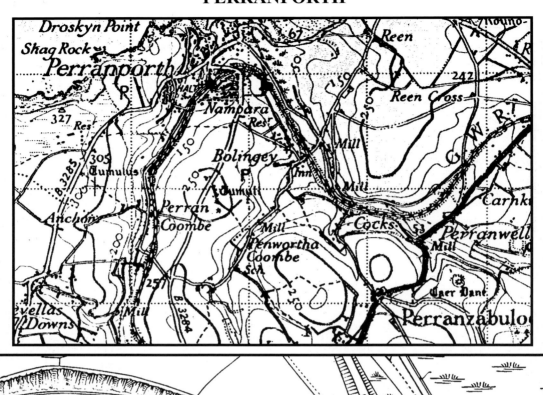

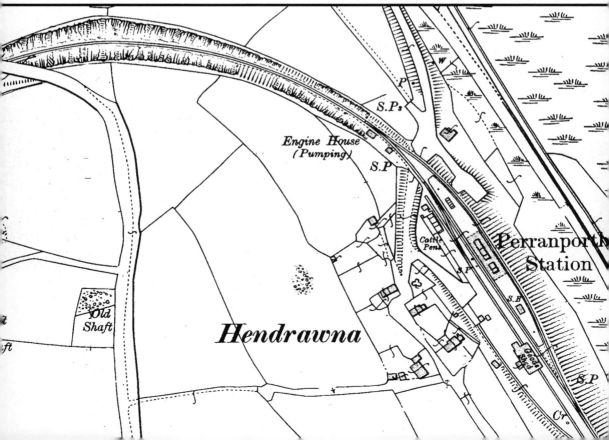

XXII. The 1946 edition is shown at 2ins to 1 mile to give the position of the halt and the station. The line drops to about 50ft above sea level before curving south.

Perranporth	1903	1913	1923	1933
Passenger tickets issued	6287	16612	23907	10249
Season tickets issued	*	*	262	510
Parcels forwarded	1209	3830	6115	11141
Coal and coke received (tons)	-	-	11	-
General goods forwarded (tons)	176	458	159	101
Other minerals received (tons)	75	133	751	853
General goods received (tons)	335	862	892	573
Trucks of livestock handled	27	64	27	9
(* not available. Seasons include holiday Runabouts.)				

XXIII. The topography made the station siting difficult. There is a deep rock cutting at the top and marshland on the right of this 1906 survey.

84. An early postcard includes a horse-drawn portable steam engine sheeted up, probably the property of the railway building contractor. The steps down from the platform to the roadway are on the left. Subways were very rare in Cornwall. There was generous provision for cattle traffic, but very little materialised. (Lens of Sutton)

85.	A slightly later postcard franked 5th September 1905 includes the bridge over the road and the adjacent signal. The station was a terminus from 6th July 1903 until 2nd January 1905, so this card must have been produced as another news item: "We now have two railmotors at our station frequently". (C.Benney coll.)

86.	A Newquay-bound Metro tank passes the pump house and water tank, probably in the 1930s. The "S" on the signal indicated that a short shunting move was permitted. It appears that the unknown photographer joined this train to take the next picture and nos 109 and 110. (Lens of Sutton)

87.   This view includes one of the once common crossings that enabled farm carts to reach the platform edge for the transfer of milk churns. The water column does not have any means of frost protection, apparently deemed not necessary in the mild climate here. (Lens of Sutton)

589   589
Gt. Western Ry.   Gt. Western Ry
Perranporth Beach   Perranporth Beach
HALT   HALT
TO
MOUNT HAWKE
HALT
THIRD CLASS
1/4½ Z Fare 1/4½ Z
Mount Hawke   Mount Hawke
FOR CONDITIONS SEE BACK HH

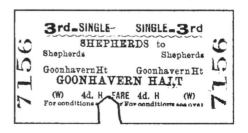

7156   7156
3rd-SINGLE-   SINGLE-3rd
SHEPHERDS to
Shepherds   Shepherds
GoonhavernHt   GoonhavernHt
GOONHAVERN HALT
(W)   4d. H   FARE 4d. H   (W)
For conditions   For conditions see over

88.   Seldom photographed is the washing apron used when cleaning out cattle wagons. The one seen in picture 84 has been heavily limewashed by railwaymen as a hygiene measure. No. 4588 is about to leave for Chacewater on 26th September 1956. (H.C.Casserley)

89.   Perranporth at 5.5pm on 3rd August 1959: a wet Bank Holiday Monday! Nos. 5546 and 5539 have arrived on the 4.39pm from Chacewater and no. 5515 is approaching with the 4.35pm from Newquay. It seems that a crew change is about to take place. The 23-lever signal box was in use throughout the life of the line. (P.W.Gray)

90.   Mr Henry Morgan was the last station master and is collecting tickets on the final day of traffic. There had been a staff of seven in 1903, but it was down to five in 1938. DMUs were used only in the final months. (K.Young)

GOONHAVERN HALT

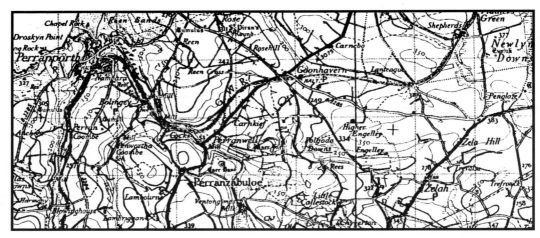

XXIV. The name refers to "Downs with Summer fallow land". The 1946 edition at 1ins to 1 mile shows the proximity of the halt to the community and also includes the next station at Shepherds.

91.   The halt was on the north side of the line and was photographed in 1922. It was opened on 14th August 1905. A lamp was provided at the top of the path; all three were tended by the guard. (LGRP/NRM)

SHEPHERDS

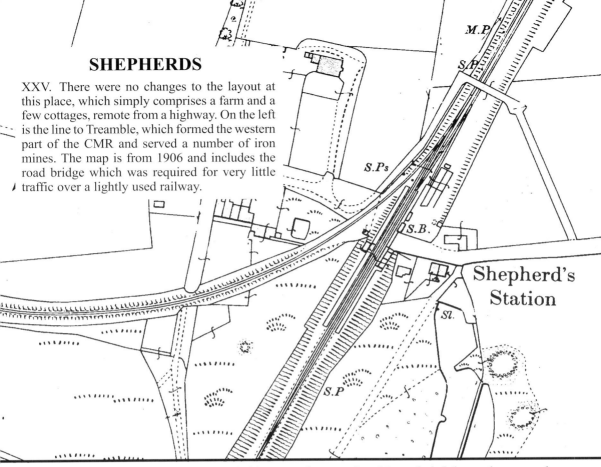

XXV. There were no changes to the layout at this place, which simply comprises a farm and a few cottages, remote from a highway. On the left is the line to Treamble, which formed the western part of the CMR and served a number of iron mines. The map is from 1906 and includes the road bridge which was required for very little traffic over a lightly used railway.

M.P

S.P

S.Ps

S.B.

Shepherd's
Station

Sl.

S.P

92. A staff of four or five was recorded between the wars, but this excluded the track gang and their supervisor. On the platform is the stationmaster in frock coat, two of his men and a customer. (Lens of Sutton)

93.   A 1947 panorama includes the cattle dock and apron, plus the signal controlling the Treamble branch. This carried public goods traffic until 1905, but minerals only until closed in 1917. The track was lifted for use elsewhere in World War I. The branch opened again for wagonload traffic on 16th February 1926, but was little used. It seems to have been last used in 1949, but official closure of the 3¾ mile branch was not until 1st January 1952. There is now little trace of the station or the branch. (LGRP/NRM)

Shepherds	1903	1913	1923	1933
Passenger tickets issued	Opened for Passenger Traffic 1905	5474	6999	5470
Season tickets issued		*	138	94
Parcels forwarded		1404	1422	1505
Coal and coke received (tons)		-	10	-
General goods forwarded (tons)	619	1646	427	149
Other minerals received (tons)	242	560	233	9211
General goods received (tons)	828	1008	739	178
Trucks of livestock handled	-	59	73	66

(* not available. Seasons include holiday Runabouts.)

94.   The branch signal is off as a trolley heads for Treamble, towing a grass cutter, in August 1948. Note that an unpainted concrete signal post was considered appropriate for the ringed goods signal. The gradient post indicates 1 in 60 down the branch, which once ended near the coast after one reversal.
(P.J.Garland/R.S.Carpenter)

A 1005

SINGLE **2nd**

PERRANPORTH
TO
TRURO

FARE 2/6 (W)

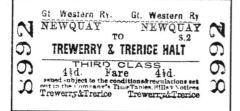

Gt. Western Ry.   Gt. Western Ry

NEWQUAY   NEWQUAY
TO   S.2
TREWERRY & TRERICE HALT

THIRD CLASS
4½d.   Fare   4½d.
Issued subject to the conditions & regulations set
out in the Company's Time Tables, Bills & Notices
Trewerry & Trerice   Trewerry & Trerice

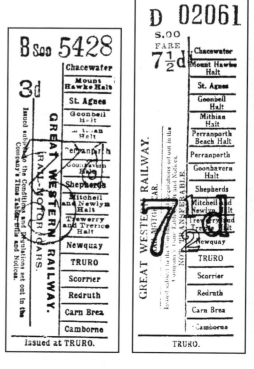

B soo 5428

3d

GREAT WESTERN RAILWAY.
(RAIL-MOTOR CARS.

Issued subject to the Conditions and Regulations set out in the
Company's Time Tables, Bills and Notices.

Chacewater
Mount Hawke Halt
St. Agnes
Goonbell Halt
Mithian Halt
Perranporth
Goonhavern Halt
Shepherds
Mitchell and Newlyn Halt
Trewerry and Trerice Halt
Newquay
TRURO
Scorrier
Redruth
Carn Brea
Camborne

Issued at TRURO.

D 02061

S.00
FARE
7½d.

GREAT WESTERN RAILWAY.

Issued subject to the Conditions and Regulations set out in the
Company's Time Tables, Bills and Notices.

NOT TRANSFERABLE

7½d

Chacewater
Mount Hawke Halt
St. Agnes
Goonbell Halt
Mithian Halt
Perranporth Beach Halt
Perranporth
Goonhavern Halt
Shepherds
Mitchell and Newlyn Halt
Trewerry and Trerice Halt
Newquay
TRURO
Scorrier
Redruth
Carn Brea
Camborne

TRURO.

95.   The branch signal was still off when the photographer moved to record the other end of the station. The timber platforms and almost everything else remained unchanged to the end. (P.J.Garland/R.S.Carpenter)

96.   The guard waits for the cameraman to complete his task on 17th August 1958. The three coaches behind no. 4587 seem to fit the platform almost exactly. (A.E.Bennett)

97.   A single camping coach was brought here each Summer in the years 1954-61. Beyond it is the road bridge which was grossly over-specified; it appears to be capable of spanning five tracks. The massive signal box housed only 23 levers and remained in use until line closure. However, only 14 levers were used. (C.Benney coll.)

MITCHELL AND NEWLYN HALT

98.   The first halt comprised a complex wooden structure on the east side of the bridge over the road and it was opened on 14th August 1905. It was more than a mile from both of the villages it purported to serve. (C.Benney coll.)

99.   A simpler and more durable structure was erected on the other side of the bridge, this being so durable that it could still be seen in 2001. (C.Benney coll.)

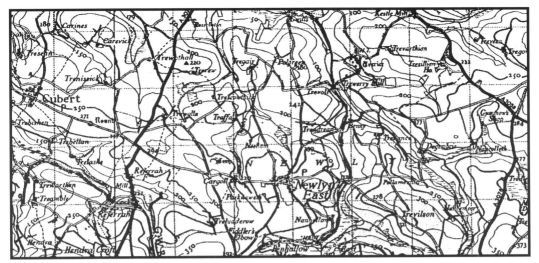

XXVI. The halt is lower centre on this 1946 map at 1ins to 1 mile. East Wheal Rose had a siding in the early years, about ¼ mile east of the halt. This map continues from no. XXIV and includes the remainder of the branch to Treamble on the left. The GWR line deviated only slightly from the CMR route. The Lappa Valley Railway was built on the trackbed between East Wheal Rose (east of the halt) and Benny (one mile to the north). East Wheal Rose had been the southern terminus of Treffry's tramway from Newquay.

LAPPA VALLEY RAILWAY

100.   The railway ends at a turntable behind the train, which is standing in the station at Benny Halt. The run-round loop is obscured by the men and the workshop is accessed from the point on the right. No. 1 *Zebedee* is an 0-6-4PT, but was built as an 0-6-2T by Severn Lamb in 1974. (P.G.Barnes)

XXVII. The one mile long 15ins gauge line from Benny Halt to East Wheal Rose was opened on 16th June 1974. The former mine site now has various leisure activities including a 10¼ins gauge railway, which opened in May 1995 and which operates a "Western" class outline locomotive named *Duke of Cornwall*. Its route is marked. The circular 7¼ins track is nearby, but not shown on the map. Few halts have three platforms and all on different gauges!

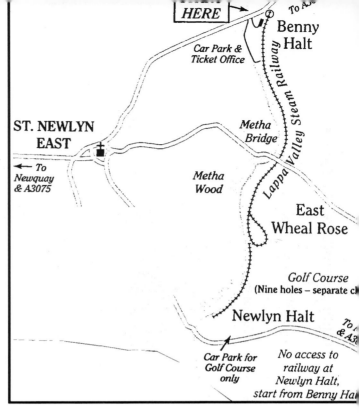

101.   Two more 15ins gauge locomotives soon arrived, these coming from Longleat. Photographed at Benny Halt on 24th April 1984 are 0-6-0 *Muffin*, built in 1967 by Berwyn Engineering, and *Gladiator* a Bo-Bo diesel by Minirail in 1960. There are ten coaches. For opening hours, telephone 01872 510317. (T.Heavyside)

TREWERRY AND TRERICE HALT

102.   The location of this halt is shown near the top of map XXVI; there was little habitation nearby, but there was an elegant bridge (right), near the mill. This was another of the 1905 batch of timber-built halts. There was a loop siding for coal traffic north of the crossing until September 1948. Nearby is the National Trust's Trerice Manor. (LGRP/NRM)

TOLCARN JUNCTION

103.   This is a northward view of the junction last seen in picture no. 59. It was taken from the road bridge (shown opposite the picture) probably in 1947. In the background is the signal box marked S.B. at the top of the map. This location was known as Lane Junction and it had its own signal box until 1888, when the curve on the right was removed; it was replaced in 1931 for engine turning purposes. The curve on the left had a 15mph speed limit. (LGRP/NRM)

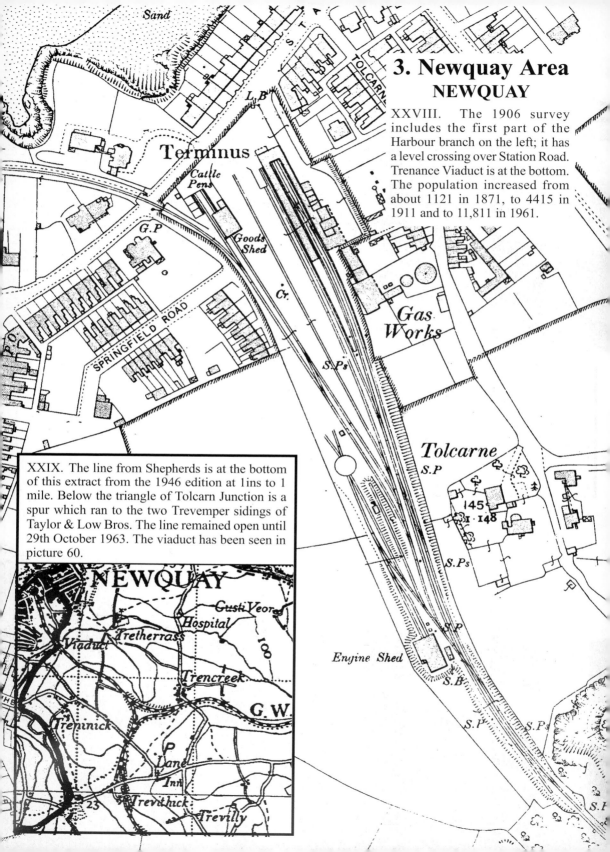

Sand

Terminus

Cattle
Pens

L.B

ST A

TOLCARN

G.P

Goods
Shed

Cr.

P.O

SPRINGFIELD ROAD

3. Newquay Area
NEWQUAY

XXVIII. The 1906 survey includes the first part of the Harbour branch on the left; it has a level crossing over Station Road. Trenance Viaduct is at the bottom. The population increased from about 1121 in 1871, to 4415 in 1911 and to 11,811 in 1961.

Gas
Works

S.Ps

Tolcarne
S.P

XXIX. The line from Shepherds is at the bottom of this extract from the 1946 edition at 1ins to 1 mile. Below the triangle of Tolcarn Junction is a spur which ran to the two Trevemper sidings of Taylor & Low Bros. The line remained open until 29th October 1963. The viaduct has been seen in picture 60.

145
I·148

S.Ps

NEWQUAY

Gusti Veor
Hospital

Tretherras

Viaduct

Trencreek

G.W

Treninick

P

Lane

Inn

23

Trevithick

Trevilly

S.P

S.B

S.Ps   S.Ps

Engine Shed

100

S.P

Newquay	1903	1913	1923	1933
Passenger tickets issued	22530	85649	102758	46891
Season tickets issued	*	*	382	1991
Parcels forwarded	27702	53666	78804	89143
Coal and coke received (tons)	1861	1569	29	-
General goods forwarded (tons)	1256	1800	1620	928
Other minerals received (tons)	11141	14430	5601	4670
General goods received (tons)	5263	7319	7664	8070
Trucks of livestock handled	48	116	18	87

(* not available. Seasons include holiday Runabouts.)

104. A "Metro" 2-4-0T waits with a Par train soon after the rebuilding of the station was completed. The island platform on the left had come into use on 7th June 1905. (M.Dart coll.)

105. Until June 1905, there was a small turntable at the far end of the original platform (right); this 1920 view includes the engine release crossover. There is a generous provision of gas lights. (LGRP/NRM)

106.   No. 4510 waits to depart for Par on 1st July 1921. A six-wheeled van leads a short bogie coach. Some of the CMR buildings are partially visible. (K.Nunn/LCGB)

107.   An April 1936 photograph includes tablet apparatus, as the line over the viaduct was not doubled until March 1946. Ths original single road engine shed was nearer the station. This signal box was in use from 1905 to 1946. (W.A.Camwell)

108.   One of the 4500 class arrives sometime in the 1930s, the roof boards suggesting that some of the coaches have been detached from an express at Par. In the background is the massive gasworks, which never had a siding. (R.S.Carpenter coll.)

109.   This is probably the train that was seen earlier at Perranporth in picture 86. The locomotive appears to be no. 1500. The GWR tried a diesel railcar here in about 1937, but the gradients were too severe. (Lens of Sutton)

110.   The rear of the same train was recorded from platform 1, which had been extended in 1928 and again in 1934. The curved parts of 2 and 3 date from the Spring of 1938. (Lens of Sutton)

111.   A late 1930s view of the extensive goods yard includes gas wagons for charging restaurant cars and a crane, which was of 6-ton capacity. By 1938 there were 27 employed at the station. The figure in 1903 had been 18. (R.S.Carpenter coll.)

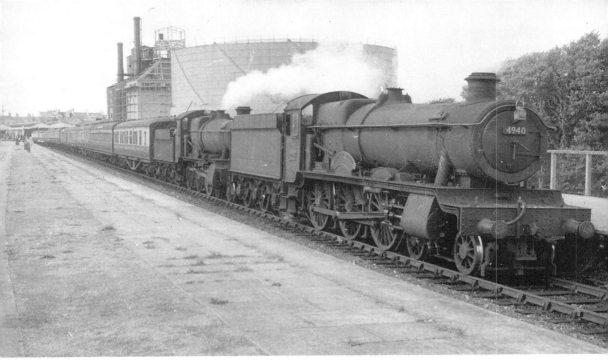

112.   All the platforms were greatly extended in 1946 as revealed in this view from August 1950 which features a holiday train departing for the North of England. The pilot engine is no. 4940 *Ludford Hall*, which was based at St. Blazey. (H.F.Wheeller/R.S.Carpenter coll.)

113.   The engine shed and turntable had gone by the early 1930s to allow extension of the sidings. This signal box was opened on 20th March 1946 and is seen in 1950. Goods traffic ceased on 7th September 1964. (P.J.Kelley)

114.   The main entrance was on the east side of the station; this is the north end, which was used for mail and parcels. It is now the only building to survive. (Lens of Sutton)

115.   No. 4673 takes water on 20th August 1961 before leaving for Par. The coaches had worked through from Falmouth via St. Agnes. Platform 3 contains evidence of the impending dieselisation in the form of a D6300 class diesel. (M.A.N.Johnston)

116. In clean green livery, Derby suburban class 116 DMU (with motor second no. W50921 leading) stands at platform 2 and forms the 18.00 service to Par on 15th June 1967. The canopy had been greatly reduced in 1964 and an extra building added. This was a travel office in 2001 and it also issued rail tickets. (G.Gillham)

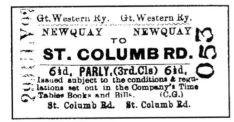

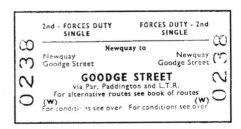

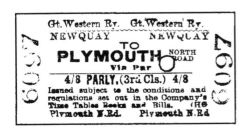

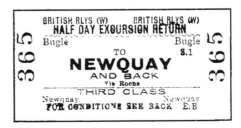

117.   The signalman collects the token for the section from St. Dennis Junction from the driver of class 118 DMU set no. P461 as it arrives forming the 14.50 from Par on 25th April 1985. The signalbox contained a 45-lever frame and dated from the March 1946 station enlargement. It closed on 11th October 1987. (G.Gillham)

118.   Nos. 50035 and 50034 stand at platform 3 with the return 17.40 excursion to Paddington on 4th October 1987. This train was organised to mark the end of locomotive hauled trains working over the branch. The last scheduled train had run the previous day. (D.H.Mitchell)

119.   Most trains used platform 1 until 1987, but subsequently its canopy was cut back to form an entrance area. A smart class 153 unit was recorded on 10th August 1998, about to run non-stop to Par at 11.20, the only train of the day to do so. It is at the former platform 2. (P.G.Barnes)

NEWQUAY HARBOUR BRANCH

XXX. This map continues from the one of the station and shows "Engine House". Above this is a building described as a store on other plans, which presumably had been the goods shed, as there was no such structure at the station until the 1905 alterations. The line through the tunnel was rope worked, the gradient being 1 in 4 to 1 in 6. Horses were employed on the harbour lines; they were last used in about 1922. The branch was officially closed in 1926, leaving the waterfront to be enjoyed by holidaymakers and fishermen, and the lower part of the tunnel to become an aquarium.

120. A postcard franked 1911 shows two ships moored at the stone-built part of the jetty, which was linked to the shore by a timber structure. The harbour was built in 1833 and the tramway was opened in 1845. It became the northern extremity of the CMR in 1873 when the jetty was completed. (M.Dart coll.)

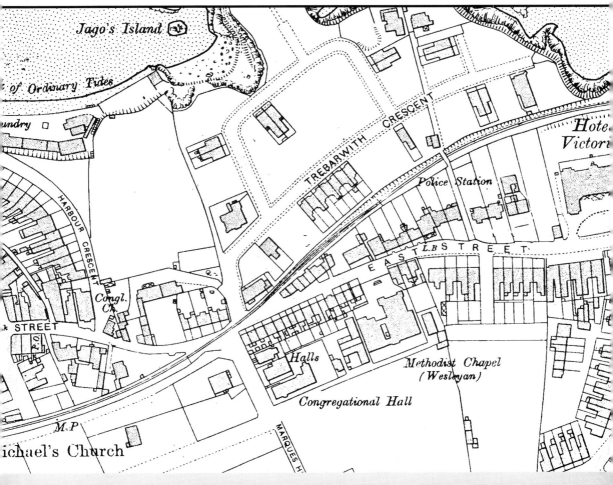

MP Middleton Press

Easebourne Lane, Midhurst, W Sussex. GU29 9AZ Tel: 01730 813169 Fax: 01730 812601
If books are not available from your local transport stockist, order direct with cheque,
Visa or Mastercard, post free UK.

BRANCH LINES
Branch Line to Allhallows
Branch Line to Alton
Branch Lines around Ascot
Branch Line to Ashburton
Branch Lines around Bodmin
Branch Line to Bude
Branch Lines around Canterbury
Branch Lines around Chard & Yeovil
Branch Line to Cheddar
Branch Lines around Cromer
Branch Lines to East Grinstead
Branch Lines of East London
Branch Lines to Effingham Junction
Branch Lines around Exmouth
Branch Line to Fairford
Branch Lines around Gosport
Branch Line to Hawkhurst
Branch Lines to Horsham
Branch Lines around Huntingdon
Branch Line to Ilfracombe
Branch Line to Kingswear
Branch Line to Lambourn
Branch Lines to Launceston & Princetown
Branch Lines to Longmoor
Branch Line to Looe
Branch Line to Lyme Regis
Branch Lines around Midhurst
Branch Line to Minehead
Branch Line to Moretonhampstead
Branch Lines to Newport
Branch Lines to Newquay
Branch Lines around North Woolwich
Branch Line to Padstow
Branch Lines around Plymouth
Branch Lines to Seaton and Sidmouth
Branch Line to Selsey
Branch Lines around Sheerness
Branch Line to Shrewsbury
Branch Line to Swanage *updated*
Branch Line to Tenterden
Branch Lines to Tiverton
Branch Lines to Torrington
Branch Lines to Tunbridge Wells
Branch Line to Upwell
Branch Lines of West London
Branch Lines around Weymouth
Branch Lines around Wimborne
Branch Lines around Wisbech

NARROW GAUGE
Branch Line to Lynton
Branch Lines around Portmadoc 1923-46
Branch Lines around Porthmadog 1954-94
Branch Line to Southwold
Douglas to Port Erin
Kent Narrow Gauge
Two-Foot Gauge Survivors
Romneyrail
Southern France Narrow Gauge
Sussex Narrow Gauge
Vivarais Narrow Gauge

SOUTH COAST RAILWAYS
Ashford to Dover
Bournemouth to Weymouth
Brighton to Worthing
Eastbourne to Hastings
Hastings to Ashford
Portsmouth to Southampton
Ryde to Ventnor
Southampton to Bournemouth

SOUTHERN MAIN LINES
Basingstoke to Salisbury
Bromley South to Rochester
Crawley to Littlehampton
Dartford to Sittingbourne
East Croydon to Three Bridges
Epsom to Horsham
Exeter to Barnstaple
Exeter to Tavistock
Faversham to Dover
London Bridge to East Croydon
Orpington to Tonbridge
Tonbridge to Hastings
Salisbury to Yeovil
Swanley to Ashford
Tavistock to Plymouth
Three Bridges to Brighton
Victoria to Bromley South
Victoria to East Croydon
Waterloo to Windsor
Waterloo to Woking
Woking to Portsmouth
Woking to Southampton
Yeovil to Exeter

EASTERN MAIN LINES
Ely to Kings Lynn
Fenchurch Street to Barking
Ipswich to Saxmundham
Liverpool Street to Ilford
Saxmundham to Yarmouth

WESTERN MAIN LINES
Ealing to Slough
Exeter to Newton Abbot
Newton Abbot to Plymouth
Newbury to Westbury
Paddington to Ealing
Plymouth to St. Austell
Slough to Newbury
St. Austell to Penzance

COUNTRY RAILWAY ROUTES
Andover to Southampton
Bath Green Park to Bristol
Bath to Evercreech Junction
Bournemouth to Evercreech Jn.
Cheltenham to Andover
Croydon to East Grinstead
Didcot to Winchester
East Kent Light Railway
Fareham to Salisbury

Guildford to Redhill
Reading to Basingstoke
Reading to Guildford
Redhill to Ashford
Salisbury to Westbury
Stratford upon Avon to Cheltenham
Strood to Paddock Wood
Taunton to Barnstaple
Wenford Bridge to Fowey
Westbury to Bath
Woking to Alton
Yeovil to Dorchester

GREAT RAILWAY ERAS
Ashford from Steam to Eurostar
Clapham Junction 50 years of change
Festiniog in the Fifties
Festiniog in the Sixties
Isle of Wight Lines 50 years of change
Railways to Victory 1944-46
Return to Blaenau 1970-82
SECR Centenary album
Talyllyn 50 years of change
Yeovil 50 years of change

LONDON SUBURBAN RAILWAYS
Caterham and Tattenham Corner
Charing Cross to Dartford
Clapham Jn. to Beckenham Jn.
Crystal Palace (HL) & Catford Loop
East London Line
Finsbury Park to Alexandra Palace
Kingston and Hounslow Loops
Lewisham to Dartford
Lines around Wimbledon
London Bridge to Addiscombe
Mitcham Junction Lines
North London Line
South London Line
West Croydon to Epsom
West London Line
Willesden Junction to Richmond
Wimbledon to Beckenham
Wimbledon to Epsom

STEAMING THROUGH
Steaming through Cornwall
Steaming through the Isle of Wight
Steaming through Kent
Steaming through West Hants
Steaming through West Sussex

TRAMWAY CLASSICS
Aldgate & Stepney Tramways
Barnet & Finchley Tramways
Bath Tramways
Bournemouth & Poole Tramways
Brighton's Tramways
Bristol's Tramways
Burton & Ashby Tramways
Camberwell & W.Norwood Tramways
Clapham & Streatham Tramways

Croydon's Tramways
Dover's Tramways
East Ham & West Ham Tramway
Edgware and Willesden Tramway
Eltham & Woolwich Tramways
Embankment & Waterloo Tramw
Enfield & Wood Green Tramways
Exeter & Taunton Tramways
Greenwich & Dartford Tramways
Hammersmith & Hounslow Tramw
Hampstead & Highgate Tramway
Hastings Tramways
Holborn & Finsbury Tramways
Ilford & Barking Tramways
Kingston & Wimbledon Tramway
Lewisham & Catford Tramways
Liverpool Tramways 1. Eastern Rou
Liverpool Tramways 2. Southern Rc
Liverpool Tramways 3. Northern Rot
Maidstone & Chatham Tramways
Margate to Ramsgate
North Kent Tramways
Norwich Tramways
Portsmouth's Tramways
Reading Tramways
Seaton & Eastbourne Tramways
Shepherds Bush & Uxbridge Tran
Southampton Tramways
Southend-on-sea Tramways
Southwark & Deptford Tramways
Stamford Hill Tramways
Twickenham & Kingston Tramwa
Victoria & Lambeth Tramways
Waltham Cross & Edmonton Tran
Walthamstow & Leyton Tramway
Wandsworth & Battersea Tramwa

TROLLEYBUS CLASSICS
Croydon Trolleybuses
Bournemouth Trolleybuses
Hastings Trolleybuses
Maidstone Trolleybuses
Reading Trolleybuses
Woolwich & Dartford Trolleybuse

WATERWAY ALBUMS
Kent and East Sussex Waterways
London to Portsmouth Waterway
West Sussex Waterways

MILITARY BOOKS
Battle over Portsmouth
Battle over Sussex 1940
Bombers over Sussex 1943-45
Bognor at War
Military Defence of West Sussex
Military Signals from the South Co
Secret Sussex Resistance
Surrey Home Guard

OTHER RAILWAY BOOKS
Index to all Middleton Press stat
Industrial Railways of the South-
South Eastern & Chatham Railw
London Chatham & Dover Railw
War on the Line (SR 1939-45)

BIOGRAPHIES
Garraway Father & Son
Mitchell & company